Oct/ 16 /0 7

D0502340

A gift for:

Alex

From:

Mom (Tonya)

Alex 9 years, 10 mths

God Thinks You're
Wonderful!

*A collection of encouraging thoughts
from the published works of*

Max Lucado

ILLUSTRATED BY CHRIS SHEA

BOK5070

For Jack and Marsha Countryman.
God thinks you're wonderful, and so do I.
MAX LUCADO

To my dad, Bill Givens,
with "such happiness."
CHRIS SHEA

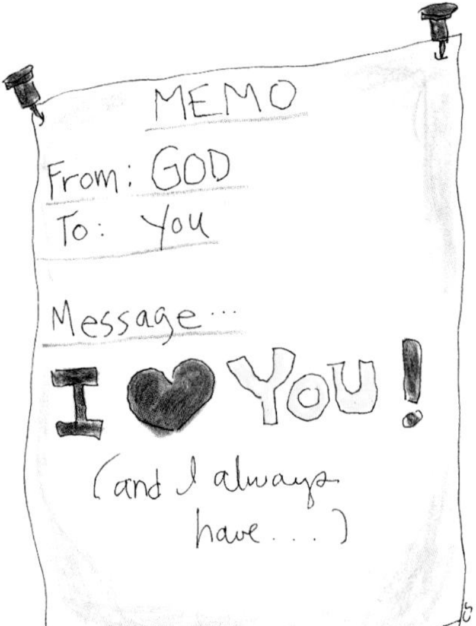
MEMO
From: GOD
To: You
Message...
I ♥ YOU!
(and I always have...)

God is fond of you . . .

If he had a wallet,

your photo would be in it.

If he had a refrigerator,

your picture would be on it.

He sends you flowers

every spring

and a sunrise

every morning.

good morning

Whenever

you want to talk,

he'll listen.

I'm always listening

He can live anywhere

in the universe,

and he chose

your heart.

x — I AM here

Face it, friend.

He's crazy about you.

20

By the way,

it may be difficult

for you

to believe that

God knows your name . . .

but he does.

Written on his hand.

Spoken by his mouth.

Whispered by his lips.

Your name.

I have written your name

on my hand.

Isaiah 49:16

your name

Your name

Joy

☆ your name

Blessings
Available

Peace
Love
Happiness
Parents
Kids
grandKids
popcicles
Kittens
Sunsets
Carrots
sun
moon
stars
pie
teachers
friends
storms
flowers
trees
dogs
intelligence
wonder
God
angels
Jesus

Try to
place in →

Our hearts are

not large enough

to contain the blessings

that God wants to give.

So try this.

The next time a sunrise

steals your breath . . .

or a meadow of flowers

leaves you speechless . . .

remain that way.

Say nothing and listen

as heaven whispers,

"Do you like it?

I did it just for you."

If we give gifts

to show our love,

how much more

would he?

He could have

left the world

flat and gray . . .

but he didn't.

He splashed orange

in the sunrise . . .

and cast the sky

in blue.

And if you love

to see geese

as they gather,

chances are

you'll see that too.

Did he have to make

the squirrel's tail furry?

Was he obliged

to make the birds sing?

And the funny way

that chickens scurry . . .

or the majesty

of thunder

when it rings?

Why give a flower

fragrance?

Why give food

its taste?

Yummy!

Could it be

he loves to see

that look

upon your face?

So promise me

you'll never forget . . .

that you aren't

an accident

or an incident . . .

you are a gift

to the world,

a divine work of art,

signed by God.

You knit me together

in my mother's womb.

Psalm 139:13

You were

knit together.

You weren't
mass-produced.
You aren't an
assembly-line product.

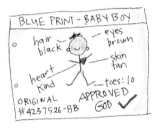

You were

deliberately planned,

specifically gifted,

and lovingly positioned

on this earth . . .

by the

Master Crafts-Man.

Bloom here!

He thinks you are

the best thing

to come down the pike

in quite a while.

You can do it!

Turn to the sidelines;

that's God cheering

your run.

Look past the finish line;

that's God

applauding your steps.

I Love You

xxoo
God

God is for you.

Had he a calendar,

your birthday

would be circled.

If he drove a car,

your name would be

on his bumper.

If there's a tree in heaven,

he's carved your name

in the bark.

Heaven - 2002

actual un-retouched photo

Maybe you don't want

to trouble God

with your hurts.

But . . .

"he cares about you"

(1 Peter 5:7).

There, there...

He is waiting for you,

to embrace you

whether you

succeed or fail.

Your heavenly Father is

very fond of you

and only wants to share

his love with you.

MEMO

Blessed be

the LORD your God who

has delighted

in you. . . .

1 Kings 10:9 NKJV

Untethered by time,

God sees us all.

Vagabonds and ragamuffins all, he

saw us before we were born.

And he loves what he sees.

Flooded by emotion,

overcome by pride,

the Starmaker turns to us,

one by one, and says,

"You are my child.

I love you dearly.

I'm aware that

someday you'll turn from me

and walk away.

But I want you to know,

I've already provided

a way back."

You have captured

the heart of God.

He cannot bear to live

without you.

God's dream is

to make you right

with him.

Sins

Faults

Mistakes

Love's
Eraser

And the path to the cross

tells us exactly how far

God will go to call us back.

It is not our love for God;
it is God's love for us
in sending his Son
to be the way
to take away our sins.
1 John 4:10

"Can anything make me

stop loving you?" God asks.

"You wonder how long

my love will last?

Watch me speak your language,

sleep on your earth,

and feel your hurts.

Find your answer

on a splintered cross,

on a craggy hill.

That's how much

I love you."

God does more

than forgive our mistakes;

he removes them!

We simply have

to take them to him.

You can talk to God

because God listens.

Let a tear appear

on your cheek, and

he is there to wipe it.

He has sent his angels

to care for you,

his Holy spirit

to dwell in you . . .

his church

to encourage you,

and his word

to guide you.

As much as you want

to see him, he wants

to see you more.

If you want

to touch God's heart,

use the name

he loves to hear.

Call him "Father."

He thinks

you're wonderful!